For Aidan, whose kindness and gentle nature inspire me
—ACK

To my family and my beloved Eli
—RT

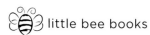 little bee books

Text copyright © 2019 by Allison Crotzer Kimmel
Illustrations copyright © 2019 by Rotem Teplow
All rights reserved, including the right of reproduction in whole or in part in any form.
Manufactured in China   TPL 0123
First Edition   10 9 8 7 6 5 4 3 2
Library of Congress Cataloging-in-Publication Data
Names: Kimmel, Allison Crotzer, author. | Teplow, Rotem, illustrator.
Title: The eternal soldier: the true story of how a dog became a Civil War hero / by Allison Crotzer Kimmel; illustrated by Rotem Teplow.
Other titles: True story of how a dog became a Civil War hero | Description: New York, NY: Little Bee Books, [2019]
Identifiers: LCCN 2018046131 | Subjects: LCSH: United States—History—Civil War, 1861–1865—Juvenile literature. |
Dogs—War use—Juvenile literature. | United States. Army. | Pennsylvania Infantry Regiment, 11th (1861–1865)—Juvenile literature. |
BISAC: JUVENILE NONFICTION / History / United States / Civil War Period (1850–1877). | JUVENILE NONFICTION / Animals / Dogs. |
JUVENILE NONFICTION / Social Issues / Friendship. | Classification: LCC E468.9 .K55 2019 | DDC 973.7—dc23
LC record available at https://lccn.loc.gov/2018046131
ISBN 978-1-4998-0863-6
littlebeebooks.com
For information about special discounts on bulk purchases,
please contact Little Bee Books at sales@littlebeebooks.com.

THE ETERNAL SOLDIER

THE TRUE STORY OF HOW A DOG BECAME A CIVIL WAR HERO

WORDS BY
ALLISON CROTZER KIMMEL

ILLUSTRATIONS BY
ROTEM TEPLOW

little bee books

Sallie's life as a soldier began in a basket.

A man from town brought Sallie to us in the 11th Pennsylvania Volunteer Infantry as a gift. Captain Terry shook his head, pushing the basket away.

"But every unit needs a mascot," the man said.

The little bull terrier pup shivered as I peered into the basket at her.
"You're not a spy sent from Johnny Reb, are you?" I asked her.

The pup barked and nearly tumbled out of the basket. We laughed, and immediately we knew—she was one of us already.

Brindle fur with streaks of brown and black swirled all over her like a patchwork quilt. She was as pretty as an apple tree in full bloom. We called her Sallie.

We took to Sallie right away. She reminded us of our families and our lives before the war.

Like a good friend, she never wanted more from us than we could give. So we shared our rations—fresh milk, soft bread, bits of meat—and she only took what she needed.

It wasn't long before she knew every beat on the drums, every note on the bugle. She recognized the notes of reveille as the morning roll call. Sallie made it to the line faster than any other soldier.

In battle, Sallie stood firm beside me and the color guard beneath the shadow of our flag, the most dangerous place. The Confederates fighting us aimed their weapons at anyone holding our colors, and that was usually me.

But I was not afraid, and neither was Sallie. She stood right next to me there on the firing line, barking at the rebels.

After each battle, we marched onward to the next one. Our feet were heavy and tired, but Sallie always kept our spirits light.

One trek took us not to combat, but to an important meeting with fellow Union troops.
There onstage, President Lincoln himself stood ready to review his army.

Sallie led the 11th past the president. I'll never forget how the man,
face creased with worry, raised his tall hat to salute our Sallie.

Two months after the president acknowledged Sallie, we joined other Union troops fighting on Oak Ridge outside Gettysburg.

We fought for two hours. Sticky, hot weather covered us all, Union and Confederate alike. Smoke from the continued firing of guns hung heavy in the air, leaving behind a weary, gray fog.

We fought until we ran out of bullets. Then, I was struck in the arm. And there on Oak Ridge, I fell. One of our men grabbed the colors as our squad retreated. He ran to accompany the rest of the men as the colonel had ordered us to fall back to Gettysburg.

The battlefield around me grew empty. The loneliness among the silence made everything suddenly still.

I could not fall back. I noticed some of our men lying near me.

We were wounded. We were fading. The rest of the 11th had to leave, but we stayed, not knowing what would become of us.

When the smoke began to clear, I saw Sallie standing right beside me as if we were back on the firing line.

"Go to safety, Sallie," I urged her.

But Sallie sat down on the ground in front of me. She licked the wound on my arm to stop the bleeding. We could hear the explosion of cannons, the yell of the rebels growing closer, but still, Sallie wouldn't leave her post beside us.

Somehow, I knew she wouldn't leave.

And she didn't.

The battle thundered for two more days. All that time, Sallie never left our side. She paced back and forth between us.
She licked the wounds of the living so that they might heal, and guarded the bodies of the dead so that no rebel could touch them.

Men cried out for their mothers, for their wives, for people who weren't listening. But Sallie listened. And so, she went to them.
She lay beside them. She waited and kept watch over them.

Four days after her duty as a watchdog over the
battlefield had begun, Captain Cook, an officer
from a Massachusetts unit, found Sallie.

He tried to pet her, but she would not let him.

She had not eaten or had water for quite some time, but Cook knew what Sallie wanted. His men carried all of us, Sallie's soldiers, off of the Oak Ridge dirt. Only then did she let Cook take her to rejoin the 11th.

Soon, I was healthy enough to carry our colors again, and Sallie returned to duty, too. On her first day back, a soldier from another unit tried to retreat from our line. Sallie responded by tearing the seat out of his pants. She knew good soldiers never abandoned their men.

Almost two years after Gettysburg with the war nearing its end,
we marched to Hatcher's Run, Virginia, to engage the enemy.

The night before that battle, Sallie
could not rest. She cried out all night.
She had never done that before.

During our first charge into the fight the next day, Sallie fell in the shadow of the colors. She did not cry out. Death had spared her pain.

But our pain remained.
The dust from battle stung our tears as
we buried her there on the battlefield.

More than twenty-five years would pass before the 11th Pennsylvania Volunteer Infantry met again at Gettysburg. We dedicated a monument on Oak Ridge to all of our soldiers. We did not forget Sallie.

At the base of our monument sits a bronze statue of the 11th's bravest soldier. She just happened to be a dog.

Visitors share their rations with her, leaving biscuits by Sallie's statue to this day. They leave pennies with the heads facing up so President Lincoln can still salute her.

There, her head rests against her paws. Her eyes are open in the direction where the rebels once came from, and, ever a loyal soldier, she keeps an eternal watch over the field for her men.

Author's Note

In May of 1861, a special member joined the farmers, coal miners, and lumbermen who, as part of the 11th Pennsylvania Volunteer Infantry, became soldiers. These young men from rural Pennsylvania immediately took to the four-week-old pup who was presented as a gift to them.

They named her in honor of a real woman, Sallie Ann, who was known as the most beautiful girl in nearby West Chester. Though the pup shared Captain Terry's quarters, Sallie fit in among all the men and seemed to have no particular favorite. She chose to march beside a different soldier daily during drills. She was also able to distinguish her soldiers from those of different units. She was fiercely loyal, always returning to her squad, and she made it her duty in battle to bark at the Confederate rebels, whom the men of the 11th proudly claimed Sallie hated.

Sallie became as much of a soldier as any other member of the 11th. She responded to different bugle calls throughout the day, which were used to structure all Civil War soldiers' duties. These bugle calls told the troops when to get up and get to the line (reveille), when it was time for drills, when the end of the day was (taps), and they also gave orders across the noisy battlefield. Taps is still played at military funerals to signal the end of that soldier's duty.

She also recognized the 11th's flag, called "colors," and knew the importance of staying beside it in the confusion of a Civil War combat zone. Smoke from gunfire and cannons clouded soldiers' vision, so the primary role of the colors was to stay visible and keep a unit together by providing its soldiers with a boost in morale. If the colors advanced, so, too, did the unit's soldiers. If the colors fell or were captured by the enemy, this meant humiliation and defeat.

Like a proud flag-bearer, Sallie never abandoned her unit. She had four litters of puppies during the war. Each time, she left only to give birth and returned to duty the next day. Soldiers from the 11th sent these puppies home to their families or gifted them to local residents.

Sallie marched with her men to many notable battles, among them the Second Battle of Bull Run, Fredericksburg, Antietam, and Chancellorsville, but her most famous performance on the front line came at Gettysburg, where she was credited with keeping many of her soldiers alive and comforted as the battle raged on for days. When she was finally found, she was nearly dead. Her dedication to them inspired her inclusion in the 11th's monument at Gettysburg, which was built in 1890. More than two decades after the war had ended and Sallie had given her own life in battle, her men still remembered her fondly. Colonel Coulter described Sallie's eyes as being "full of fire and intelligence" (Coulter 1867), and many visitors to Gettysburg National Park feel a similar kinship when they see Sallie's battle-weary eyes forever captured in bronze.

Sources

Coulter, Richard. "Sallie," *Republican and Democrat* (December 18, 1867): Greensburg, PA.

Stouffer, Cindy and Cubbison, Shirley. *A Colonel, a Flag, and a Dog*. Pennsylvania: Thomas Publications, 1998.

Zucchero, Michael. *Loyal Hearts: Histories of American Civil War Canines*. Virginia: Schroeder Publications, 2013.

Reenactors of the 11th Pennsylvania Volunteer Infantry, 11thpvi.org